That's Entertainment

That's Entertainment:
Field Notes on Love, Politics and Movie Musicals

Alan Gann

LITERARY PRESS
LAMAR UNIVERSITY

Copyright 2018 © Alan Gann
All Rights Reserved

ISBN: 978-1-942956-52-5
Library of Congress Control Number: 2018932679

Cover Photo by Bruno Minkley

Lamar University Literary Press
Beaumont, Texas

For Indigo—
I believe you would have liked these poems.

Recent Poetry from Lamar University Literary Press

Bobby Aldridge, *An Affair of the Stilled Heart*
Michael Baldwin, *Lone Star Heart, Poems of a Life in Texas*
David Bowles, *Flower, Song, Dance: Aztec and Mayan Poetry*
Jerry Bradley, *Crownfeathers and Effigies*
Jerry Bradley and Ulf Kirchdorfer, editors, *The Great American Wise Ass Poetry Anthology*
Mark Busby, *Through Our Times: Occasional Poems 1960-2017*
Paul Christensen, *The Jack of Diamonds is a Hard Card to Play*
Chip Dameron, *Waiting for an Etcher*
William Virgil Davis, *The Bones Poems*
Jeffrey DeLotto, *Voices Writ in Sand*
Chris Ellery, *Elder Tree*
Ken Hada, *Margaritas and Redfish*
Michelle Hartman, *Disenchanted and Disgruntled*
Michelle Hartman, *Irony and Irrelevance*
Katherine Hoerth, *Goddess Wears Cowboy Boots*
Michael Jennings, *Crossings: A Record of Travel*
Gretchen Johnson, *A Trip Through Downer, Minnesota*
Ulf Kirchdorfer, Chewing Green Leaves
Janet McCann, *The Crone at the Casino*
Jim McGarrah, *The Truth About Mangoes*
Erin Murphy, *Ancilla*
Laurence Musgrove, *Local Bird*
Laurence Musgrove, *One Kind of Recording*
Godspower Oboido, *Wandering Feet on Pebbled Shores*
Carol Coffee Reposa, *Underground Musicians*
Jan Seale, *The Parkinson Poems*
Steven Schroeder, *the moon, not the finger, pointing*
Vincent Spina, *The Sumptuous Hills of Gulfport*
Glen Sorestad *Hazards of Eden*
W.K. Stratton, *Ranchero Ford/ Dying in Red Dirt Country*
Wally Swist, *Invocation*
Loretta Diane Walker, *Desert Light*
Dan Williams, *Past Purgatory, A Distant Paradise*
Jonas Zdanys (ed.), *Pushing the Envelope, Epistolary Poems*

For information on these and other Lamar University Literary Press books go to
www.Lamar.edu/literarypress

Acknowledgments

I am grateful to the editors of the following anthologies and journals for publishing some of the poems in this collection:

Ain't Gonna Be Treated This Way: Celebrating Woody Guthrie
Poems of Protest & Resistance 2017
CyberSoleil Literary Journal
Panoplyzine
Poetry of the American Southwest #3: Weaving the Terrain
Red River Review
Texas Poetry Calendar
Wordfest Anthology 2017

CONTENTS

11	Overture and Prologue
13	100 Remembered Words: June 12, 1982—Arches to the North Rim
15	When America Was Great
16	That's Entertainment
17	100 Lost Words
18	Ellis County Fall 1973
19	Cowboy Code
21	100 Words for Max
23	Hide and Go Seek
25	Clang Clang Clang
26	100 Words for Boxing Day
27	Guinness
29	Based on a Play by George Bernard Shaw
30	100 Morning Words
31	Perseids
33	Predictable
34	100 Words while Driving
35	Buttons
37	Pink Sweaters and Poodle Skirts
38	100 Words after Dropping By
40	Okra Stew
41	When the Eternal Spring is Over
42	100 Word Letter from Caitlyn
43	Doing It
44	Hat Dance

45	100 Word Allergies
46	Fire for Emily
47	Chumps and Love
48	100 Sleepless Words
50	Ghazal for a Hushed Tongue
51	No Reason Needed
53	100 Word Hurricanes
54	In a Book I Read And Cherish
55	What's the Name of his Other Leg?
57	400 Words until Easter
62	Your Mountain
65	Bali Hai
66	100 Blue Words
68	Pendulums
70	The Emcee
72	100 Words on Sweet Grackle Love
73	Pulse
74	In Rick's Café Americana
75	100 Word Prayer
76	Nymph
77	Let the Sunshine
79	100 Words on 420
81	Wounded
83	Dismantling My Library
85	100 Golden Words
86	Transmission
89	L'chaim

Overture and Prologue

somehow fifteen seconds
and two sharp trailing whistles over a black screen
contain 13 billion years before people began cultivating fields
on a tiny coastal island left behind when ice bergs receded

with four and a quarter orchestral minutes left
for the exchange of beads, waves of immigration
building and crumbling apartments
four and quarter orchestral minutes
shifting saturated hues over a single delicate drawing
vertical lines indeterminate and abstract
fuchsia to harlequin to atlantic blue
chartreuse and tangerine stretching and stretching
until any observant observer intuits eventual resolution
so no one is surprised when skyline finally emerges

and still we have another minute flying above
docks and roads and tenements
cars turning toward destinations we will never know
Yankee Stadium fixes the location
then fingers snapping
before a slow zoom down to teaming streets
to basketball courts where bored Jets wait for the mayhem
bored Jets play it cool

all in one seamless pan before the ballet begins
before Jets arabesque and plié
own the streets with entrechats and brisé
at eight minutes and twenty seconds they meet Bernardo
and it's on for six and half more minutes
choreographed chase and skirmish
revealing that Sharks also know how to snap in time
balançoire and battement glisse

chí-chí-chí turn and scamper
graffitied walls baited traps
shifting advantages and garbage dumps
violins and woodwinds
punctuating bongos brass and timpani

until fourteen and a half minutes in
finds everyone back at the chain-linked courts
where this dance all began
twirling tossing punched in time
sirens and cops and Officer Krupke
speaks first line of real dialog—*break it up*
so the story can begin

100 Words Remembered:
June 12, 1982—Arches to the North Rim

Driving across the Hopi reservation
at 3:30 in the morning
everyone
including the driver
woke
when the car bounced to a stop.

Headlights illuminated a saguaro cactus
limbs lifted
in either greeting or surrender.

Cooling desert air
crackled against bare arms.
No Peterbilts barreling on
signaled any way back.

Never occurred to us
we could have driven
off a cliff
broken an axel
or that the car
might not get us to the canyon

because we were invincible—
recent grads living it up
on a cross country boondoggle
armed with enough cold beer
and leftover pizza
to outlast any darkness.

When America Was Great

god looked like my grandfather
president like a smarter me
banker a richer me
and the police just like me

so I could vote
Humphrey-McGovern-Carter-Mondale-Dukakis
not noticing how black friends
spoke just like me only around me

but now my banker is a computer screen
almost anyone can be president
cops come in all colors shapes and sizes
and god
well the last I looked
she was pulling out her braids and yelling
don't lay your trip on me

That's Entertainment

Musicals!
Mama loved spangled girls dancing with tuxedoed gents
Rogers and Astaire tapping up a spiral staircase
Gene Kelly dressed as a sailor
Judy Garland parading down the avenue
Corny love stories with silly misunderstandings

So after Sunday comics my sister and I
scanned TV listings usually channel 33
often rolling late past late
so we'd have to beg school night endings

While Kathy and I got into our pajamas
Dad fiddled with the antenna loop
Mom made popcorn and Cokes with lemon

Then squeezing onto the sofa
beneath one of Grandma's quilts
I often fell asleep
only to wake with the morning sun
and an irresistible tune on my lips

100 Lost Words

I am not the first
to sleep where the Bright Angel
meets the Colorado

not even first atheist
to find god
when stars and silence overwhelm.

I could describe how sky turned purple
and completely miss the point.
It is enough that the sun has set

and I have hiked beyond the campgrounds
with no agenda or flashlight.
Not exactly lost

I rest on a fallen log
feel stones surrendering the day's heat.
Coyote on the opposite bank

drinks aware but unstartled by my presence.
I could probably find my way back—
really should, but can't quite figure out why.

Ellis County Fall 1973

Because it was the week before Halloween
Because it was warm enough outside that no one wore a jacket
Because our parents were inside watching Mary Tyler Moore and Bob
    Newhart
Because brooding clouds shrouded then revealed a moon so full
    of itself
Because a tractor slept in the barn beneath our feet
Because Jackson swiped a pack of Marlboros from the Winn Dixie
Because none of us had ever drunk so much basement wine
Because the only thing dumber that one 13 year old boy is a dozen
Because Jeff said *I will if you will*
Because our sneakers squeaked against the shingles
Because we could just make out Sara's shadow through her curtains
Because I was the youngest they let on the roof
Because Terry clucked at me like a chicken
Because when Jimmy took off his jeans, his underpants seem to glow
Because Playboys were stashed safely in the tree fort
Because laughter is a gypsy charm and witch's curse
Because I wanted to make an impression and chances are rare
Because I couldn't think why not
Because we heard a train whistle dying away
I surrendered to a sky full of ghosts
and jumped

Cowboy Code

Mom's weekend away
so donuts for breakfast
Coke with lunch
scrambled cheesy eggs for dinner
and singing cowboys before a late bedtime

Dad pins a tin star to my chest
tacks Cowboy Code to the mantle
We load our cap pistols
and blast away at fleeing bandits
though Sherriff Autry never fires a shot

Dad peppers the night with trivia
Roy Rogers in his first movie role
Only time he pointed a gun at Gene Autry
Those bad guys are the other Sons of the Pioneers

And we sing along with *The Old Corral*
So Long Old Pinto
Silent Trails
Down Along the Sleepy Rio Grande

boo when big city gangsters
kidnap the lounge singer
cheer when Gene and Roy and Sons of the Pioneers

team up to foil their scheme with a cattle stampede
and soon a song together

And I cover my eyes when the movie ends—
rescued damsel embraced by the sheriff
for a big ol' yucky kiss

100 Words for Max

Nobody signed-up
for the Children's Poetry Workshop,
but at three before four
Miracle Max
spins through the door
and they all come tumbling after.

Max
unafraid of messy words
and poetry
cheerfully writes himself
a learner
video gamer
cheetah chasing prey
excited every day.

You wouldn't know it,
but beneath Max's green shirt
a mighty scar
holds everything together
because at ten years
his heart has been twice broken
twice repaired.

Miracle Max rolls on the carpet
gold fuzz clinging to pants.
Doesn't care
can't help it—
carpet is soft and springy
and like life itself
tickles just a little.

Hide and Go Seek

M I crooked letter crooked letter I

One Mississippi tribe
band of Choctaw

Two Mississippi myths
riverboat gamblers calling aces and eights
smiling slaves wishing they were
back in Dixie away away

Three Mississippi civil rights workers
one black, two white
arrested in June 1964
buried in a nearby dam

crooked letter crooked letter I

Four Mississippi
one too many
between lit fuse and firecracker tossed

Five Mississippi
deep inhales and exhales
before I talk back to Mama

Six Mississippi tourist traps
The Gen. Steven D. Lee Education Museum
Vicksburg Battlefield
Soldier's Rest at Cedar Hill
Natchez Plantation Tour
Fort Massachusetts on the Gulf
Cannons at Corinth

humpback humpback I

Seven Mississippi rests stops
between Alabama and Louisiana
where we never stopped
cause Mama said
we didn't need to go that bad

Eight Mississippi cousins
at the family reunion and learning
some great-grandparents owned others

Nine Mississippi musicians
Robert Johnson Howl'n Wolf John Hurt
Leontyne Price Tammy Wynette Conway Twitty
Muddy Waters Bo Diddly and some guy named Elvis

Ten Mississippi
ready or not

Clang Clang Clang

First night of winter break
and everyone in town must have stayed up late
because for five days every cousin and friend
friends of cousins and kids we didn't even know
ran up and down the streets
through Winn Dixie, Sears, and Belks bargain basement
banging out undefined polyrhythms
singing in no identifiable key
at the top of enthusiastic lungs
until mothers emptied aspirin bottles
downed liberal glasses of medicinal eggnog.

Spontaneous parades marched in and out of houses
(forgetting to close wreath-decorated doors)
spoons pounding against baking pans
strings of jingle bells spun wildly above our heads
garbage can lids and empty paint buckets
all marked the coming and goings of an invisible trolley
clanging towards the manger on Christmas Eve.

100 Words for Boxing Day

Thing I like about Santa Claus
is he never talks about Jesus

thing I like about Jesus
is he never asks about work

thing I like about my job
is not working for a living

and thing I like about living
is its insistence on poetry.

Thing I like about the Easter Bunny
is he's never stingy with his chocolate ears

and thing I like about my ears
is pressing them against your chest

and thing I like about beating hearts
is never knowing when they will stop

and thing I like most about dying
is its insistence on poetry.

Guinness

It is not St. Patrick's Day
and I am drinking a Guinness

Bartender tips the empty
pulls the tap
and while slowly straightening the glass
fills pint near to overflowing

To be a real country
you must have a beer
a sport is helpful
airlines and weapons optional
but you must have a beer

He watches the cascade—
bubbles separating from liquid
build the creamy head
and after a moment's appreciation
tops the pint with a foamy crown
presents it
to the scarred and polished bar

Four ingredients: barley and hops
water from St. James's Well
and yeast with a two century pedigree

Naturally eyes are drawn down
toward beauty—resist keep chin up
focus above and beyond
look out the window or through the mirror

After milling and mashing
separation, boiling, and fermentation
everything is allowed to settle
and find its balance

With straightened spine and lifted elbow
never leaning forward
hoisting glass to lips
breaking the seal
sweet-roasted brew honors my tongue
a tinge of bitter finds the back of my throat

Based on a Play by George Bernard Shaw

After Eliza tells Henry he shall never see her again
and Mrs. Higgins tells her son that he'll have to do without
a commercial comes on and Mom switches TV off
hustles my sister and me up to brush our teeth
and then to bed

Over breakfast we discuss Eliza's future
and Mom tells us what Shaw explained in the Epilogue---
Pickering underwrites her marriage to the hopeless Freddy
They open a flower shop—struggling before success

But now-a-days a smart independent lady
wouldn't accept charity or feel compelled to marry
and she'd work her way up
earning her partnership in the flower shop

Perhaps as an additional warning to my sister
who was beginning to show an interest in boys
Mom pointed out how Henry used chocolate to manipulate
and ultimately resistance proves Eliza's a lady

When we read the play in sophomore English
Ms. Perdue had a substitute show the movie
and I wondered if my sister knew
what Mom artfully concealed—after the final commercial break
a most unladylike Hepburn returns to fetch his slippers

100 Morning Words

when there's no cold pizza
and neither of you wants
to face the Sunday morning sun
not yet

but there's no eggs or pancake mix
no orange juice or bagels
when you both need to get out of bed
pee
brush your teeth and shower alone

dump the cartons
of leftover Pad Thai
red curry
Mussaman potatoes
and saffron rice
into a microwavable dish

serve steaming
on warm flour tortillas
with salsa verde and chips

bring breeziest conversation to the table
make sure the coffee is not bitter
a smooth burn
fragrant and strong enough
to point the way home

Perseids

*Be still and listen, because you're drunk
and we're at the edge of the roof* —Rumi

        The bottle was full
        when we climbed the oak
        and dropped to the roof
        lay on our backs
        watching pieces of the sky
        flare and break loose

        You point at the centaur
        and the bears
        I start reciting

                constantly risking absurdity

*You know the brightest stars
aren't even stars*

                *very tired, very merry,
                back and forth all night*

That's Jupiter beneath the swan

                *the whiskey on our breath
                could make a small boy dizzy*

        when giggling
        you lift your tank top

Always wanted a peak at these,
haven't you?
Well take a good look—
it's gonna be the only one you ever get

        I almost roll off but you reach over
        and take my hand

                        Knock Knock
Who's there?   *Doctor*
Dr. Who?   *Precisely*

        Laughing-gasping-laughing
        Leaning-rising-leaning
        until four wobbly legs
        support two spinning heads

        I toss the empty
        high over my left shoulder
        and we do not hear it land
        This must be a sign

        So tomorrow we will wake
        hungover and bruised—
        perhaps discover something cracked
        but tonight
        drunk on moonless sky and rhyme
        we fly

Predictable

as cheap laughs follow buffoonery
as infatuation follows moonlight
as farce follows mistaken identity

Predictable
as dirty looks in the Thackeray Club
as tuxedos and tails
as a sarcastic manservant

Predictable
as Ginger's glance
as music rising and Fred's singing
as reluctant acceptance of a proffered hand

Predictable
as a slapped cheek dancing cheek to cheek
as a gondola ride through the canals
as wedding bells and the bridal suite

Predictable
as Mom taking Dad's hand
for a turn round the family room
to an orchestral reprise over closing credits

100 Words while Driving

Morning rush hour
half-mile from entrance ramp to exit.

Shuffling SUVs and sedans
F150s and eighteen wheelers
6 lanes
to merge left at 60 miles per hour
while the purple Caddy
sidesteps 4 lanes right
then veers off toward Ft. Worth.

Two Peterbilts headed for Waco or Austin
wedge themselves
among the anonymous Camrys and Accords.

Sipping coffee
checking phones
texting replies
ignoring rain
heads bobbing to private playlists.
She's reviewing notes for the morning update.
He's making up excuses.

It is clearly impossible
except bosses don't give a damn.
We are every weekday professionals
and this is our dance.

Buttons

had everything needed to save the world—

Ban the Bomb
Swords into Ploughshares
Peace is Progress

Brenda worked in the faculty printing office
Jamal owned presses and cutters
I bought blanks at a craft shop near campus
Jimmy brought the weed
and Vanessa swiped bottles of wine from her parent's cellar

No Means No
My Body My Choice
Shirley Chisolm For President

met in the backroom of Student's for Democratic Action
read week-old copies of the Free Press and Village Voice
cut out images and slogans du jour

Ban the Klan
Meat is Murder
Love Your Mother Earth

sometimes after a particularly rousing night
Brenda and I would find an empty study room and make out
but she always felt like she was betraying the sisterhood

Live Simply
Subvert the Patriarchy
Homosexuality is not a Crime

setup between quad and cafeteria
handed out our buttons
collected signatures
and promoted the next rally against

ERA Now!
Free Tibet
Black Power is People Power

but Brenda graduated and moved to San Fran
so she could be a real dyke
then Jamal got busted
and Vanessa's dad put a lock on the cellar door

Legal Smoke
Make Groovy Groovy Love
Donald Duck for President

and when I came back from summer break no one in the SDA
pushed my buttons in exactly the right left way

Pink Sweaters and Poodle Skirts

Couple of gin and tonics
while watching Danny and Sandy sing and dance
their way through high school and street races
prompts a giggly mom's confession—she was a Pink Angel
with three girls from down their street—
matching pins and sweaters worn to the Harvest Festival
made other girls jealous
guaranteed a dance card filled with hunky seniors

Once, when parents went out of town
planned slumber party at her house
but instead of staying up late and doing each other's nails
took a bus into Nashville
to see Duke Ellington at Pearlie's Supper Club

Turns out they were only white folks
in a rowdy smoke-filled bar
Tuxedoed doorman set them a table by the stage
and at the end of the night wouldn't take their money
Were lucky last bus ran a little late
so four dawdling girls made it home before dawn

Parents never found out
so they never got in trouble
could never tell anyone greatest secret ever

100 Words after Dropping By

a kiss
was the thing
furthest from my mind
but I saw you sitting on the deck
in that hand hewn glider
and imagined licking
bitter coffee and dark chocolate
from your lips

I imagined
with just a tinge of guilt
your unfettered tan

when you lifted your t-shirt
I forgot how to breathe
until your fingers
slipped inside my waistband
and inhaled a chill
rushing through clenched teeth

veterans
of chance encounters
we are long immune
to dawn's embarrassment

still I blushed
at the chuckle you shared
with the Waffle House waitress
when she greeted us
Some morn'n, huh?

Okra Stew

Some use olive oil to sweat away the sheen
but we melt a glob of bacon fat
toss in onion, garlic, handfuls of chopped okra
cover and simmer, uncover and stir
until slime's just a memory
chunks rough-skinned and tender

Now stew it up with tomatoes, ham hocks
bell and cayenne pepper, couple jarfuls of stock
bit of everything in your spice drawer
two bay leaves
little more cayenne
and if you got one in the icebox
a catfish head really rounds out the broth

Turn that heat way down, pour yourself a glass
maybe touch more cayenne
go sit on the porch and let it simmer.

Most folks throw in some shrimp
but we got crawdads big as daddy's boot
so put a few in to boil with a big old pot of rice
add a final garnish of cayenne
and get ready to go dancing tonight.

When the Eternal Spring is Over

Worldly and bored
falling in and out of love
the way flowers blossom so they can shed their petals—

yet when real love
innocent forget-all-my-troubles
cheating-at-cards love
strikes like lightning
his only question
is rent or buy?

I shall go away with you...
sleep in your bed...
When we fight
it will be in all the columns...
You'd give me up...

Marriage may be forever
but it doesn't cure the passing of years
and like the poorest slight-of-hand
delightful laugh
gives way to a second child
world war
a wandering eye—
Yes, Gaston...it begins again.

100 Word Letter from Caitlyn

Dear Taylor Dear Pink Dear Beyonce

all over America
12 year old girls just like me
wearing our flirty t-shirts
and boring underpants
grab a hairbrush

stand in front of the mirror
and sing your songs

practice making your moves
our moves
wish hair or hips
chest or eyes
were just a little more

until my mom yells
hurry up we're going to be late

and I pull on tightest pair of jeans
wishing they were just a little tighter
sharpie colored sneakers
over favorite mismatched socks

go bopping down the hall
as the crowd screams
for one more song

Doing It

When I was 5 and Adrienne 6, she took my hand and led me into a closet. We turned the lights off, took our clothes off, kissed on the lips, and thought we had done it. Until she heard Jimmy's older sister got pregnant *doing it*, went crying to her mother, and we both got a good talking to.

In 4th grade I learned about Tab A and Slot B, and the girls said gross and giggled when a boy pistoned a finger in and out of a tunneled palm.

In Junior High I learned about baseball, and only a homerun counted as *doing it*.

We stood in a circle and watched Val half swallow a banana, then pull it out again and again. We knew that wouldn't count as *doing it*, but would be way better that a handful of second base.

I don't remember *doing it,* not the first time I actually did it. It was at church camp, so everyone by the lake was either drunk or high. I remember a bonfire, and she took my hand, led me behind some rocks. I do remember the next day Adrienne teasing me that maybe we finally earned that good talking to.

Hat Dance

When you dance with Gene Kelly
you're going to fall
in love

so consider yourself forewarned
if a sad-faced seaman
with divided passions
should wander into your courtyard
followed by a familiar tune

but beggar girl in folkorico
is unschooled
in the rules of rhythmic seduction

so they prance around the fountain
de-da de-da de-dada
de-da de-da de-dada

until music fades
and her sailor
feeling better if still a bit confused
wanders off
with wistful wave goodbye
deaf to the first crack
in a six year old heart

100 Word Allergies

you are the riot of wild flowers
sting of a thousand bees
buzzing stamen to pistil to hive

I am the bear jonesing for your honey

you are my watery eyes
phlegmy sneeze
cough creeping down
and lower still

dividing and subdividing
as bacteria go bacterial
viruses going viral
sinuses going sinusoidal

I tell everyone that rash is poison ivy
but we both know
you are the only itch I scratch

you are malicious ragweed
encroaching on my trail
shooting higher with each summer rain
reason I curse first hard freeze

but only by your absence
can I breathe again

Fire for Emily

Today we burn like *hope*
sunrise where fire *is the thing*
consuming itself to fly or fall *with feathers.*
Yours is the name *that perches*
claws dug in sinew turned bluenotes *in the soul*
to take flight *and sings*
like smoke spirals up and up following *the tune*
smolders through mist and clouds *without*
spark or hearing *the words*
trembling uncertain *and never stops*
to wonder anything burns *at all.*

Chumps in Love

Chumps lay down a good dollar
for a solid gold watch
sold out of a Broadway suitcase.
Chumps suffer fourteen year engagements
or believe in chemistry.
Chumps want to get over love
when it isn't what they imagined.

Chumps never see the trap door
until after they've fallen—
take the unwinnable wager,
find ear full of cider.
Chumps will lose their heart
trying to win a bet.

But sometimes luck really is a lady
chumps roll a natural
tie the knot in the middle of Times Square—
win the wager without even knowing
they laid their markers down.

100 Sleepless Words

Once
maybe twice every night
and the trick
is to make it there and back
without really waking up
without stubbing a toe
disturbing the light sleepers
stepping on the cat's tail
or missing the bowl

but too often
having avoided all the traps
just as head sinks into pillow
feel that lightest tug

day's regret
did I forget
should have said
bills and bank accounts
what will I do when

like a ball of yarn
tossed by the cat
relationships time and money
become an impossible tangle

loosening one thread
knots another
while the alarm
creeps closer and closer

Ghazal for a Hushed Tongue

Watching Orion climb the night, we feel compelled to whisper.
Milky Way puts city lights to shame, listen for the whisper.

Sun pushing through stained glass projects a multihued stigmata.
Under judgmental gaze of saints, we speak to God in whispers.

Dim-lit hospital room, a loved one is about to die.
Lean forward, kiss and stroke their hand, share secrets in a whisper.

By day we can walk above the dead sharing a glass of wine.
But after dark, only fools and graveyard drunks do not whisper.

Books are holy things, by volume and page their spells are woven.
Librarians stare, their presence reminding me to whisper.

Siamese once worshiped, bronze statues glyphed with smooth exaltations.
Curled in your lap, they purr and listen only if you whisper.

A waltz so our bodies meet and mingle, band and lights are low.
Hand on waist, three steps turn, speak my name urgent in your whisper.

No Reason Needed

When infatuation meets impossibility
no other reason needed
for Donald O'Connor to sit Gene Kelly down
and let the mayhem begin

slip on a banana peel
plop down on a sofa, climb the wall
get fresh with a headless prop
slapped and all to make 'em laugh

When infatuation meets impossibility
no other reason needed
for Cyd Charisse to lock eyes with Gene Kelly
and the set dissolve

dance through a smoky landscape
mauve and orange
pure white train unfurling
in time to choreographed breezes

When infatuation glimpses possibility
no other reason needed
for Gene Kelly to wave the taxi away
and embrace the deluge

dance with twirling umbrella
climb a light post pause beneath a pouring spout
drops glimmering in the night
perfectly tapping toes
splash in time

100 Word Hurricanes

on some unscheduled night
soon after Epiphany
we slice ripe pomegranates
squeeze and strain the seeds

pale winter sun
reminds me of prim pink curtains
hanging in Grandma's kitchen

unimaginable if you'd seen her
dip crawdads in hot sauce
and step fast to the fiddler's run

boil juice with sugar
add lime for a little zing
pour crimson syrup into a Mason jar

let it rest
until the Tuesday before Lent

swirl with rum and OJ over ice
call torrential rains
winds whipping waves higher than high tides
until drenched and exuberant
we take our last sip just before midnight

In a Book I Read and Cherish

Christmastime and cold, *I went to the woods*
to escape twinkling lights, *because I wished*
to see stars and cry, *to live*
where if I did not build the fire, I might die, *deliberately*
recalling dinners with Mom and Dad and *to front*
at fifty-five I was an orphan. *Only the essential*
tiny tent, beans, coffee, pen, paper, *facts of life*
which easily fit into my pack *and see*
if words would come, *if I could not learn*
to catch my dinner and sleep alone—*what it had to teach*
of rising and paw prints and changing light *and not*
frantic filling of my barrel, so *when I came to die*
I would *discover*
something sufficient, unknown if *I had not lived.*

What's the Name of His Other Leg?

I know a man with a wooden leg named Smith.

1.

after all the dancing penguins
treacly remedies and one man bands
after supercalifragilistic suffragettes
ancient banker get the expialidocious

and we have gotten the joke
learned our lessons
taken hold of our lives again
so it is time for the turning of the vane
winds coming dead on from the west

time to repack
hat stand
floor lamp
mirror
plant
and of course the tape
that takes the measure of everything
all back into the valise

2.

fired Father finally free tells a joke so funny
senior partner dies laughing
and all the other black clad bankers
celebrate with a day in the park

fired Father finally free calls the children down
no time to say goodbye no time for tears
so many pigeons to feed
let's go fly a kite

fired Father invited back into the fold
red carnation rewarded for a happy corpse
newest partner smiles and answers yes
doesn't hear the rattling of the chains

recently unfettered Father
just as he discovers the joy of silly songs and kites
turns the key and locks the shackle round his own ankle
ensuring he will never again have the time

400 Words until Easter

1. Maundy Thursday

Thursday before Easter
and youth group met in the basement
for fellowship—
pizza and ping pong
rapping bout temptation and sin.

To practice our Christ-like humility
we washed each other's feet.

I'm probably only sophomore
to ever touch Jennifer Pickerel's feet.
She giggled
as I placed pink-painted toes
in the warm perfumed water

shifted a little
flowered dress riding up and up
parted knees just a bit
so I could glimpse smooth blue cotton.

Was I going to hell—
not for looking
but wondering

if Mary of Bethany wore a bra
if Jesus got a boner
looking down her tunic.

2. *Good Friday*

Until I was 12 years old
I assumed it was good
because we got out of school early

giving us time to pack
before midnight
when we piled into the car
for the 8 hour drive
to Macon
where most of my cousins lived.
My sister and I tried
to stay awake, but usually conked out
before hitting the city limits.

I'd never realized
that only his death was essential—
that Jesus didn't have to rise

so when we woke
with Georgia sun in our eyes
all we had to do was believe
and Good
seemed a mighty small word.

3. Holy Saturday

Schrodinger's Savior
could have rolled that stone away
(just another miracle)
but chose to stay
neither dead nor reborn
waiting for an angel

did he slowly stretch
rub aching shoulders
run thin fingers
over still raw scars
wince and for a fully human moment
curse hammer wielding soldiers
nails and holy lance

perhaps conjured water
to slake unholy thirst
took solace
in balm of wine
perhaps alone in the dark
touched himself and smiled

I like to imagine Jesus
reveling in unscheduled hours
no clamoring disciples

no line of infirmed
seeking his touch
no moneychangers in need of his wrath

4. *Easter Morning*

Not yet dawn
and only Jesus and I have risen

He could have made coffee
but didn't
hidden eggs but didn't
turned OJ into mimosas but didn't

and I could still be dreaming
walking into class wearing only underpants

but evidently
need to experience miracle
to believe and be saved

tell Jesus the only thing I want saved
is time
Suggest he do the lawn—
won't wake the neighbors
using our push-reel mower

Hey-soos—I mean Jee-zes
calls me a racist

heads down to the pond
skips a rock to the other side
walks across
retrieves his stone
skipping back

Your Mountain

it's your mountain—
rocky sometimes snowcapped peak
woods meadows cliffs
long forgotten trails

your mountain
everything on it yours—
acorn nibbling deer budding flowers
hawk nesting in oldest sycamore

all yours
every cave
every creature inside
mice possums

some years a wolf some a bear
nesting swallows in the crevices
walking stick dung beetle
damsel and dragonfly

hasn't always been your mountain
but is today
and will be tomorrow and tomorrow
until the day it no longer is

your mountain
aquifer-chilled creeks and cattail stands
your sunfish and water snakes
lizards toads and turtles

lucky you
patches of blackberries and honeysuckle
fourteen apple trees
and spring-ripe with morels

all yours
even the dragon in her impossible lair
centuries asleep on a hoard of rubies and gold
dwarves underground mining veins of sliver

some say winds are unfettered
but these are your breezes
hints of peach blossom
barely cool enough to make a summer bearable

your mountain
the always green grove
of thirty-seven oak and thirty-seven ash
high too high above the tree line

all yours
elves sprites fairies

dancing the grove
moving seasons and the sun

your mountain all yours
to climb or not
catalogue flora and fauna or not
terrace and farm or not

you could choose
a not-too-warm sunny afternoon
hike the low trail
look down on the village

but the world needs wild and unexplored
as much as you need exercise
while high above the clouds air grows thin
loki whispers in heisenberg's ear

where synapses twirl and spin
but it's your mountain all yours
and like every choice, every challenge
like every coyote's howl

if deer find a greener pasture
if breeze quits blowing
if dragon takes to air
there's nothing you can do
because none of it belongs to you

Bali Hai

where dreams come to dream
silhouette topped by cloud-shrouded peaks
so seabees can imagine
island girls and coconut liquor
flowing
dancing
free
shrunken heads
grass skirts
boar-tusk bracelets
ripe for the groping

shifting light
prejudices clash with passion
rules get bent and bullets resolve

Bloody Mary travels back and forth
knows difference between trinkets and love
sings of aspiration and reverie
without which there are no misty veils

100 Blue Words

Revived
heart pumping again
but he was blue
not sad
skin and hair
color of his stonewashed Levis

friends evenly divided
between sorry and cool
not that it really mattered
he was blue
left handed
made good grades except in history
and being blue didn't help
memorizing which battle
was fought on which date

in college
he became a thing
women lined up to join
blue phallus club
only a few
signing on as frequent flyers

worked 65 hour weeks
at a tech startup
sold for 65 million
retired to the beach
armed with green cash
and a platinum card

Pendulums

Because somebody has to be first
Because gravity doesn't care about alternate facts
Because daughters grow into mothers
Because power never gives itself away
Because color lines are made to cross
Because sometimes money trumps love
Because breastfeeding isn't exhibitionism
Because sometimes boys are really girls
Because you can get your own damn coffee
Because we'd only pay Hillary 70% of what we paid Bill
Because stairs don't have ramps
Because being first means being better, smarter, nicer, prettier
Because it's harder than you think to carry the dead vote
Because sometimes blue lives trump black
Because only Nixon could have gone to China
Because glass ceilings are made to shatter
Because pussy hats are pink
Because emails can be hacked
Because some girls are really boys
Because hope never hung a door
Because no person is illegal
Because being first means being safer
Because it's okay to spell check your protest signs
Because even progressives who know better speak louder to the blind
Because walls make prisoners of us all

Because some babies grow up neither girl nor boy
Because in private, civil rights veterans call Obama the safest Negro
Because football players get away with rape
Because pendulums swing both ways
Because going backwards isn't an option anymore
I don't know how
Because I was born white and middle class and male
Because skin and bones and bank accounts fit like well-worn jeans
Because I walk down dark streets and never think rape
Because little league, YMCA, and Pop Warner were assumed
Because what I know will never burn as hot as what she feels
Because I graduated with degrees instead of debt
Because I never feared the cops
Because good intentions don't cut it
Because my boss never whistled at my butt
I write and write and write, critically unqualified to finish this poem

The Emcee

decadent god
paints his face dons his tuxedo
clanks under the spotlight and sings
two ladies two ladies
lacy bloomers and leather bustiers
money money money
pelvic thrust grope and grin and wink
sacrifices himself on the altar stage
kit kat club his temple

willkommen
outside it is winter
jokes keep worshipers warm
in here life is beautiful
so hot
laugh to forget
even the orchestra is beautiful
je suis enchante
fight to keep their clothes on
and tonight we may lose the battle
bada-boom

voyeur god
non-aryan eyes
see what's smoldering
beneath flirt and champagne
swastikas and broken hearts

tomorrow belongs to them not us
impotent god
who created whom
through the funhouse mirror
difficult to tell

100 Words on Sweet Grackle Love

Any self-respecting male
knows to claw and caw
until territory is marked and unchallenged.
Then wait
until she casually
perhaps even accidentally
lands nearby.
Down from his perch
spreading wings and tail he struts
circling closer
until she pecks
Get back!
What kind of grackle
do you think I am?
But she doesn't fly, so he doesn't give up.
Circle, peck, circle, peck.
Sometimes he jumps the gun
and she rolls
lifts her talons
forces him squawking
to retreat.
But she doesn't fly
so circle, peck, circle, peck
until with a big hurrumph
she turns away
and lifts her rump.

Pulse

June 12, 2016

Love is love Disco is dance And neither will ever die Throbbing lights Writhing shadows Poppers and X Pumping veins Thrust and jerk Woman or man Love is love but Bullets are bullets Minds are twisted Wheels of fate spin round and round

Strangers cry for strangers Words fired smug and justified like bullets biding their time But love is love until sweaty skin dries to salt and bus comes to carry us home A too bright sun shines through and still the heat-hate-beat goes on and on and on Because love is love Disco is Dance and neither will ever die

In Rick's Café Americana

cool mysterious Rick
risks money
shut down club
nights in jail
even his life
but not control or appearing the fool

Only Victor Laszlo
turns his back on arrogant Nazis
bar full of strangers with everything to lose
and commands the band
Play La Marseillaise
trusting an unbaptized choir to rise and follow and sing

Imagine
passion inspiring courage and faith
risking absurdity more than death
if Third Reich tenors
overpower free French trumpets

while Ilsa alone at a table for two
feels the tearing of her heart
hoping Victor understands Paris and how
when the world is on fire
rules get bent

100 Word Prayer

war should be more
than making little pieces of metal
pass through human flesh

crumbling buildings
burning fields
raping and slicing

war should be more
than nurturing soil with blood
belief that god is on our side

we don't trust your funny clothes
color of your skin
sound of foreign words

seems there's something
something inside that needs domination
so history books teach

wars my side won
made the world a better safer place
but a just war would be blind and deaf

righteous and erase all hopelessness
at least balance the scales
better and safer for my side

amen

Nymph

Whenever I get too busy *she calls*
–former lover reminding *me*
how we left clothes close *to secluded pools*
swam with mergansers and bufflehead as *a long*
afternoon disappeared into blue-gray dusk, *quiet shores*
erotic as any boudoir. *Beneath*
still hidden stars and *canopies of white oak*
deer grazed on fresh fallen acorns *and red*
turned leaves surrendered to breezes scented with *cedar.*

Whenever I get too busy all *I have*
to do is answer yes, *no need*
to check my calendar or pack a toothbrush. *Tonight*
lives a short silent walk down to the stream *(for noise*
even a whispered prayer could block the way) *no desire*
beyond bristling skin and beauty. *For that*
is the ripest berry and there is no *other life.*

Let the Sunshine

when   locks long enough
smiles wide enough
                judgement cocked   little too much
            wine and smoke strong enough
        music twirling   loud and wild enough

fringe and bandana
                granny skirts and denim vest

the whole of Central Park belongs   to your songs
outstretched hands   welcoming
                                         new age dawning

after midnight movie she shook her head—hippies are the only
ones share their sunshine and stash with a hick fresh off the bus

even being turned on   dropped out
                arrested   and in love
cannot prevent Claude
from becoming
a good soldier   except for the one time he isn't

by the time I turned 18 they hadn't drafted anyone
in a couple of years but we still had to register (inscribed
CO across my form which made the clerk laugh) still
young men were shooting and being shot
dying and buried beneath sterile white crosses

                        and only in the age of aquarius
black and white police horses   dance
     mirroring the black and white gypsy couple
                    they are unable to contain

          groovy man   just too groovy

100 Words on 420

4:20 a.m. on 4-20
and if I had any
I'd roll and smoke one
(assuming I could still find my lighter)

to still mental mice
running round and round
rattling tiny mental wheels

sunburn doesn't help
or cat's meow
paws stalk not-so-mental mice
across my brow

I google *stoned mice*
wandering mazes
giving up before they find
bitter ironic cheese

and when two chance to meet
it's embarrassing
all those noses rubbing tails erect
forehead to forehead
ear to ear to ear

hilarious videos
if I were just a few puffs over
falling down that dreamless
mickey mouseless
rabbit hole

Wounded

Walking on arthritic knees and getting laid off
Blond women crossing the screen in dishy dresses
Disrespect and the blow from a tire iron
Confident men tossing keys to the valet
Falling off the pedestal of privilege
like hopelessness

wounds
and wounded people
find their tribe compare their scars
decide who is us who is them
who to blame and how to hate

Wounded people
create myths and monuments
learn hymns and catechisms
Make-America-Build-the-Wall-
A-Christian-Nation-Great-Again
and when the time comes
light their torches and march

Of course we've all touched the hot stove
but I never faced a night
without faith in another dawn
never bore the lash

worried if flashing blue lights
meant a speeding ticket or a bullet
No one ever refused to serve my pale skin

Wounded people
know their oppressors
better than we know ourselves
create myths and monuments
learn hymns and catechisms
We-shall-Overcome-Black-Lives-Matter-
When-do-we-want-it-Now!
Time to throw off the yoke
link arms and march

I was born to oppress
so easy keeping to well-lit sides
But the heart is a devious muse
and too privileged to ever be tied to any mast
heard the siren's song
and followed beauty to the disturbing truth
If I do not help tear down the wall
do not sing the overcoming
do not link arms and march

if I remain silent
I become one of the wounding people
might as well tattoo a swastika on my head

Dismantling my Library

Ships are safe in harbor, but

cover against cover, standing at attention
wedged between Rabbit running and Rosewater pondering,
firebombs fall and Dresden crumbles—
Billy Pilgrim cannot come unstuck in time.
And Victoria Warshawski will never discover why
her friend's lawyer is lying face down in the pool.

Spiking trees with Hayduke,
sauntering through the 100 acre woods with Henry David
and it being a hummy sort of day. Drunk in Pamplona,
fishing with Santiago. Nights with Alice
growing curiouser and curiouser. Train rides seem but a blink
when searching for clues with Miss Marple and Hercules.

that's not what ships are for

and lately I feel Smiley's disapproving gaze—
J. L. Seagull want to fly, Shoeless Joe another swing,
and Atticus, dearest Atticus, needs to do
what must be done. I hear them whisper, please—
cracked spines and coffee stains,
in bathtubs, on subways, at the beach—we do not care.

So Jim Nightshade take Holly Golightly and go—
run and flirt, bought and sold, loaned out
and never returned. Sherlock deserves better
than a well-lit recliner—perhaps a penlight beneath a blanket,
backseat of family vacation, stolen minutes in the breakroom,
perhaps a riverboat down the Mississippi.

100 Golden Words

predawn tollway sign flashes
less than 5 minutes from Eldorado
just a skip and jump
from the legendary city of gold

cement mixers to the left
dump trucks to the right
pickups loaded with brown-faced men
all barreling toward Eldorado
less than five minutes away

hour earlier
fastening seatbelt before landing
looking down on neon cityscape
abstract scattering of lights
river of cars snaking their way toward the center
I could believe
every city
polished bright
paved with gold

but Eldorado is just another exit
hyper-lit yellow arches
strip malls and olive garden
iron pyrite and pink flamingo
painted gold

Transmission

from the Latin *Trans* meaning beyond across change
and *Mission* meaning to send away

metal giants marching across
stick figures
shouldering their load of electrons
bundled uninsulated
garlanded from tower to tower

look back look back look back
there
the coal burning
wind harvested
sun captured
water pulled through the dam
potential energy transformed

stand beneath and listen to the hum
hundred and thirty-eight kilovolt buzz
feel your bones rebel against
transmission

somewhere a turbine spins
so you can flip a switch
and the television

the computer
refrigerator
air conditioner
light bulb

in the end everything glows
night is meaningless
fire is meaningless

in my tiny apartment I count
two hundred and seven devices
requiring electrons to flow through wire

Mission is a town butting the Rio Grande
two in the morning prime crossing time
transfer to a dark trailer
transported beside transmission lines
set free in the glowing parking lot of an HEB

my mechanic prefers
working on manual transmissions
meshing gears is art
shifting a skill
higher gears go faster
lower gears do more work
still rich men prefer
smooth automatic rides

and the stick figures march
transformers bulging
biceps of copper and steel
tireless across the fields
beside the highways beyond the horizon
connecting source to destination
dreamers to dreams hands to purpose

let their bones own the night
double-clutch into overdrive
let their skins own the day
harvest the sun capture the wind
until the turbines spin for them

L'chaim

Only reason the fiddler keeps his balance
is because he has always kept his balance.

> Neighborhood kids played in the woods
> picked blackberries nobody owned
> and mischief was common currency.

None of the Jews drinking with Tevye
know any of the young Russians
but who doesn't like to dance and drink
and celebrate a match.

> Until I was 12
> and went to the newly integrated middle school
> I didn't even know there was another side of the tracks.

Tevye rages and stomps at the flaunting of tradition
Daughter who make her own match?
Impossible!
until he considers one hand and the other.

> When I was 13, my parents came home early
> caught me making out with a new girl
> and while we scrambled to hide our embarrassment
> heard my dad in the next room
> *I told you he wasn't queer.*

The constable is such a good man
Tevye almost wishes him a Jew
but even friendship
cannot solve a night of official mischief.

>Bronson was my first black friend. We played
on the same basketball team at the Y.
Sometimes he would bike over to my house
stay for dinner but I had no idea where he lived.

In Kiev they are doing new dances
no longer asking permission but only a blessing
so what can Tevye do except give both
and dance with his wife.

>Taught no meant no, many bases
went unstolen. Mary Ann liked me better
but asked Mark to the prom
because she heard I wouldn't put out.

And just when he thinks there is no other hand
God brings his down to rearrange the pieces—
pogroms and wars and boats to America.

>Macy's sells underwear where my tree fort used to be
and Interstate 40 runs through fields
once gold with corn
and melons filched for a snack.

Still the fiddler plays tunes
kept alive
deep in our bones.

Inspirations

Italized text in *Fire for Emily* was taken from the poem *"Hope" is the thing with feathers* by Emily Dickinson .

Italized text in *In a Book I Read and Cherish* was taken from *Walden* by Henry David Thoreau. The title comes from the poem *Going to Walden* by Mary Oliver.

Italized text in *Nymph* was taken from the poem *Blue River* by Ken Hada.

Some of these poems sprang from a viewing of these films:

West Side Story (1961 – Natalie Woods and Rita Moreno based on the Jerome Robbins/Leonard Bernstein/Stephen Sondheim play)
The Old Coral (1936 – Gene Autry, Smiley Burnette, Irene Manning, and Sons of thePioneers w/ Roy Rogers)
Meet Me in St. Louis (MGM 1944 – Judy Garland, Margret O'Brien, and Mary Astor)
My Fair Lady (1964 – Audrey Hepburn and Rex Harrison, music by Lerner and Loewe)
Top Hat (RKO 1935 – Fred Astaire and Ginger Rogers, music by Irving Berlin and Max Steiner)
Grease (1978 – John Travolta and Olivia Newton John)

Gigi (1958 – Leslie Caron, Maurice Chevalier, Hermione Gingold, and Louis Jourdan, directed by Vincente Minnelli, music by Lerner and Loewe)

Anchors Aweigh (MGM 1945 – Frank Sinatra and Gene Kelly)

Guys and Dolls (1955 – Frank Sinatra and Marlon Brando, music by Frank Loesser)

Singing in the Rain (MGM 1952 – Gene Kelly, Debbie Reynolds, Donald O'Connor, and Cyd Charisse)

Mary Poppins (Walt Disney 1964 – Julie Andrews and Dick Van Dyke)

South Pacific (1958 – Mitzi Gaynor, music by Rodgers and Hammerstein)

Cabaret (1972 – Liza Minnelli and Joel Grey, directed by Bob Fosse)

Casablanca (1942 – Humphry Bogart, Ingrid Bergman, and Paul Henreid)

Hair (1979)

Fiddler on the Roof (1971 – Chaim Topol)

www.ingramcontent.com/pod-product-compliance
Lightning Source LLC
LaVergne TN
LVHW041343080426
835512LV00006B/591